31 verses EVERY TEENAGER SHOULD KNOW

THE WAY

By
Chris Kinsley

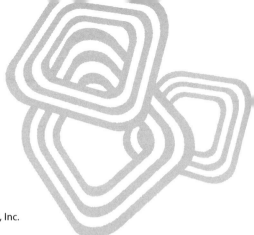

© 2008 SL Resources, Inc.

Published by SL Resources, Inc.
Student Life
2183 Parkway Lake Drive
Hoover, AL 35244

www.studentlife.com

ISBN-10: 1-935040-01-4
ISBN-13: 1-935040-01-9

31 Verses Every Teenager Should Know™

table of contents

intro

Just what is the Way? Is it a person? A movement? A revolution? A particular worldview? A system of belief? A lifestyle? A religion? The answer to all of these is yes.

In the Gospels, we find Jesus calling people, "Come, follow me." This is the same call we answer today. *The Way* is the narrow path of following Christ. The Way stands in opposition to how the world tells us to live. My purpose in writing this book is to merely skim the surface of this concept, which causes such a great disturbance, and see how it impacts not only our lives but the very nature of who we are.

I've tried to make this a little easier by breaking it up into three sections. The first contains some things that Christ Himself said as the person of the Way. The second consists of a few verses from the Book of Acts that chronicle the early days of the Way as a movement of people here on Earth. The last section is taken from the letters of the New Testament and hopefully provides further insight on just what in the world it means to live a life on the Way.

It's my prayer that God uses these verses to inspire and encourage you in your own journey on the narrow path. I hope that you will spend time pondering each of these verses and allowing them to become deeply ingrained in you. I also want to offer my own encouragement that you don't stop there. Come back to these verses repeatedly. Explore the context of the other verses surrounding them. By no means is this a comprehensive list of Scriptures about the Way. Take the time to discover others and see how the Spirit might continuously guide you into their truth.

Remember, life is a journey, not a destination. Enjoy it. Take in the sights. Make the most of every opportunity you have along the path. This is not a way of living. This is *the Way*.

Grace and blessings,
Chris Kinsley

Now that you own this incredible little book, you may be wondering, "What do I do with it?" Glad you asked . . . The great thing about this book is that you can use it just about anyway you want. It's not a system. It's a resource that can be used in ways that are as unique and varied as you are.

A few suggestions . . .

The "One Month" Plan
On this plan, you'll read one devotional each day for a month. This is a great way to immerse yourself in "the Way" for a month-long period. (OK, we realize that every month doesn't have 31 days. But 30 is close enough to 31, right?) The idea is to cover a lot of information in a short amount of time.

The "Scripture Memory" Plan
The idea behind this plan is to memorize the verse for each day's devotional; you don't move on to the next devotional until you have memorized the one you're on. If you're like most people, this might take you more than one day per devotional. So, this plan takes a slower approach.

The "I'm No Charles Dickens" Plan
Don't like to write or journal? This plan is for you . . . Listen, not everyone expresses themselves the same. If you don't like to express yourself through writing, that's OK. Simply read the devotional for each verse, then read the questions. Think about them. Pray through them. But don't feel like you have to journal if you don't want to.

The "Strength In Numbers" Plan
God designed humans for interaction. We are social animals. How cool would it be if you could go through "31:The Way" with your friends? Get a group of friends together. Consider agreeing to read 5 verses each week, then meeting to talk about it.

Pretty simple, right? Choose a plan. Or make up your own. But get started already. What are you waiting on?

verse 1

"But small is the gate and narrow the road that leads to life, and only a few find it"
(Matt. 7:14)

"Life is a journey." Ever had someone say that to you? They were probably an adult, and they probably said it after some traumatically embarrassing or heart wrenchingly tragic event in your life. They meant well. After all, they just wanted you to realize that whatever happened was not the end of the world. The event could actually build character for you in the future . . .

Well, I've got some news for you. They're right … at least about the "life is a journey" thing. (Whether or not an event builds character depends on the event and you response.) Your life is always in motion, and everyone is always going somewhere. The question is, "Where?"

Read Matthew 7:13-14. Think about your life's potential, what you can do, who you can be. It seems there's a number of paths you could take. However, Jesus tells us that's actually not the case. Really, there are only two: the broad road and the narrow road. You could take the broad road. It's easy to find and easy to follow. On this road, you can do whatever you want. The only problem, though, is that it's really no life at all. At the end of that path, you discover that the only thing waiting for you is destruction.

But that's not what Jesus desires for you. He tells you to enter through the narrow gate. (What is this talk about a narrow gate? Read John 10:7 for a hint.) In verse 14, Jesus reveals that this gate leads to a more difficult path. Not many people find it because it can only be found in Him. However, those who do find it take the only Way that actually leads to life—and not just eternal life, but an abundant and full life here on Earth as well.

Your journey begins when you choose a gate. Which gate have you chosen?

1. Which way are you currently taking in life? The broad way? The narrow Way? Describe how you know.

2. Why do you think the broad way is easy? And what's so hard about the narrow Way?

3. Write a prayer below thanking Jesus for revealing to us the two paths in life. Ask Him to continue helping you as you walk the narrow Way.

verse 2

Jesus answered, "I am the way and the truth and the life. No one comes to the Father except through me."
(John 14:6)

Do you know what it feels like to be lost? To have no idea where you are, much less how to get where you're supposed go? So lost that you're not even sure how to trace back your steps to where you began. There's absolutely nothing you can do. Unless someone comes along. Someone who knows where you are, where you're supposed to go, and how you can get there. Even better, they volunteer to show you the way. You go from being a complete slave to your circumstances to being absolutely free to reach your destination.

That's how it is with Jesus.

Ever since Adam and Eve were cast out of the Garden of Eden because of their sin, humankind has been trying to find a way back to God. If history proves anything, it's that humanity has failed completely to do this on our own. So, God took matters into His own hands and came to Earth to show us the Way. Is it that simple? Well, yes and no. This can be a tricky concept. In fact, some of Jesus' closest followers were often confused about it.

Read John 14:5-7. In these verses, it was almost time for Christ to return to the Father in heaven, yet some of the disciples still didn't get it. So, when Thomas asked Jesus where He was going and how they were supposed to know the Way, Jesus decided to make it absolutely clear. In verse six, Jesus says He is the Way. No one seeking God can do so apart from faith in Christ. When we come to Jesus, we also find the Father.

The more we get to know Jesus, the more we get to know God. And knowing God is truly the Way to life.

reflect

. Think about a time when you have been hopelessly lost. Describe how it felt. How did it feel once you finally found your way again?

. How do people try to find ways to God?

. How have you tried to find a way to God apart from Jesus? Have you found the way through Jesus Christ?

. Write a prayer below confessing Jesus as the way, the truth and the life. Repent of the different ways you've tried to find God in the past apart from Christ.

verse 3

"But what about you?" he asked. "Who do you say I am?" Peter answered, "The Christ of God.
(Luke 9:20)

Think back to when you were a kid. (Hopefully it wasn't that long ago) Remember how every day was an adventure? Remember waking up early on Saturday mornings to watch cartoons and eat cereal with more sugar than your little body could process? Then, you headed outside to all the adventures in store. Maybe you were a princess meeting her prince, or a spy secretly tasked with discovering the neighborhood's secrets. Were you a cowboy hot on the trail of some bank robbers? Or an astronaut exploring a new, faraway planet? The journey began when you took the first step outside.

As we get older, this scenario can be difficult. Not the imagination stuff—hopefully you'll always have that—but the first step thing. Older kids and adults are much more concerned about feeling comfortable and safe. We become a little less likely to blazingly pioneer a new path we've never taken. We are scared of the unknown. Yet, all we have to do to make the unknown "known" is to simply take that first step.

Read Luke 9:18-20. People throughout history have had all kinds of opinions about who Jesus is. Even while He was walking around on Earth like the rest of us, people couldn't agree on what to think about Him. When Jesus asked His disciples who the people said that He was, it wasn't because He was curious or worried that He was leaving the wrong impression. It was because He really wanted to know if they knew Him. Peter answered that question in verse 20. Jesus is the Christ of God, our Lord and Savior.

If you have questions about that whole "first step" deal, don't miss the importance of what Peter said. Confessing that Jesus is Lord is the first step on the Way.

Have you taken the first step yet?

reflect

. Why can we sometimes become less adventurous as we get older?

2. Who do you say that Jesus is?

3. What can be difficult about taking the first steps toward a journey with Christ?

4. Write a prayer below confessing to Jesus who He is to you. If you've never taken the first step of acknowledging Him as Lord and Savior, confess to God the reasons why.

verse 4

> Then he called the crowd to him along with his disciples and said: "If anyone would come after me, he must deny himself and take up his cross and follow me.
> (Mark 8:34)

Have you ever used a GPS or ridden in a car with someone who had one? They're fantastic. Anytime you want to go somewhere, you just program it in to your handy Garmin™ or TomTom®, and off you go. Along the way, a pleasant, electronic voice tells you exactly how to get where you want to go. Need something along the way? Food? Restroom? Detour? Just ask the GPS, and it's right there with an answer. Isn't it interesting that even though we are ultimately in control of where we're going, we put our trust in a little electronic box, following wherever it leads.

Read Mark 8:34-35. Jesus' call to people He met throughout the Gospels, and His call to us, is made up of just two simple words: "Follow me." Though the words are simple, Jesus makes it abundantly clear that choosing to walk that path is actually pretty hard. No one can ever accuse Him of trying to trick us by painting a picture of the Way as all sunshine and rainbows. Instead, it's a life made up of sacrifice.

When any of us chooses to answer Jesus' call and follow Him, we must deny our own selfish motives. This means that we make following Christ our priority, and that we make all of our wants, wills, and desires secondary to that. This isn't something to be taken lightly. It's not easy. It's not even something we just do once. All along the way, every morning we wake up, each moment of each day, we continually face choices of whether we're going to go where we want to go or, instead, if we're going to follow where Jesus is leading us.

Following Jesus is an all-or-nothing decision. You can't do it halfway. Are you ready to put Him above you?

reflect

. What do you think it means to follow Jesus?

2. What, in your experience, can be hard about trusting Jesus' lead?

3. What are some ways in which you need to "deny yourself" in order to follow Christ?

4. Write a prayer below confessing to Jesus how difficult it can be to follow Him. Ask for His help in denying yourself in the ways you wrote about above.

verse 5

"But seek first his kingdom and his righteousness, and all these things will be given to you as well."
(Matt. 6:33)

"Hakuna matata!" Remember that phrase? It comes from the Swahili people of Africa and literally means, "no worries." It's often used like the English phrase, "no problem."

Of course you probably know it because Timon and Pumbaa sing to a young Simba in Disney's *The Lion King*™. The young lion cub is in a self-imposed exile because of the death of his father, for which he thinks he is responsible. Simba is sad and depressed until he meets the lively meerkat and warthog duo who encourage him to forget his troubled past and live a life of "no worries." Who would've ever thought that when we sang along with this song, we were actually learning a very biblical idea?

Read Matthew 6:25-34. It's human nature to worry. We humans worry about everything. Do people like us? Are we cool? Do we listen to the right music? Is global warming destroying our planet? Am I ever going to get out of my parents' house? The list is never ending.

However, Jesus tells us not to worry. God takes care of all of His creation. He makes sure birds have enough to eat, and He dresses flowers more beautifully than the richest king. So why shouldn't you think He'll do the same for you? Basically, Jesus is trying to get you to understand that you can't control tomorrow. While you can certainly plan and prepare for the future, no amount of worrying is going to change it. You can sit around and be anxious about it all you want, but that won't make any difference.

So, what should you do instead? Seek after God. That's the way to live. Discover what is important to Him and what He would have you do. He'll take care of the rest.

Hakuna matata Christianity? Try it … You just might find you look at your faith in a whole new way.

reflect

What are some things that you are really worried about right now? What do you need to do to let God have control of them?

Why is it so difficult not to worry about the future?

In what ways are you currently seeking after God?

Write a prayer below to God about your worries. Tell Him about them. Tell Him why you're worried. Ask Him to take full control over these areas of your life.

verse

> "Come to me, all you who are weary
> and burdened, and I will give you rest"
> (Matt. 11:28)

ant to try a little experiment? Pick a day, any day. Pick one 24-hour period. Now, for that one day, try to do everything right. I mean everything. Everything you do. Everything you say. Everything you think. It all has to be exactly right. Now, you may be asking, "Whose standard of 'right' are we talking about here?" Well, God's, of course. That's right. For one day, try to live in such a manner that you do everything exactly how God wants you to do it.

Most of you just checked out. You're thinking, "Why even try? That's impossible!" And you're correct. It is. Any of us can spend our whole life, not just a day, trying to do things right, only to realize that we constantly fail and consistently mess up. Sometimes it seems the only thing we get right is doing things wrong. A life like that can really wear on a person. It's exhausting!

Read Matthew 11:28-30. Jesus came in the midst of a culture that told people the only way to God was to do right, to live according to every one of God's standards. They, like us, found they just weren't up to the task. Their constant shortcomings wore them down more and more. Can you relate?

Jesus understood this. So in verse 28, He invited all who were listening—all those tired, worn-out people—to come to Him. The yoke He asks us to bear along the way is light. Sure, the path itself is hard. We end up facing all kinds of troubles, but the burden to make it right no longer falls on us. It now rests with Christ.

The One that we follow is gentle and humble, and when we find ourselves a little road weary along the Way, He gives us rest.

reflect

. What burdens are you currently bearing that are wearing you down?

. How can the narrow Way be hard yet the yoke Jesus gives us to bear be easy?

. In what ways has Jesus provided rest for you in the past?

. Write a prayer below thanking Jesus for the rest He has provided for you in the past. Take a moment and ask Him to relieve you of the burdens you listed above that are wearing you down.

verse 7

"In the same way, let your light shine before men, that they may see your good deeds and praise your Father in heaven."
(Matt. 5:16)

When was the last time you were in complete darkness? I don't mean in your bedroom with the lights off or driving a lonely road at night. I'm talking the type of darkness you find camping in the middle of nowhere, or when a nighttime storm knocks out the electricity on your whole street. In this type of darkness, you literally can't see your hand in front of your face.

Sitting in darkness, you can find yourself hoping for even the slightest bit of light. And when you finally see it, be it a glimpse of a campfire through the trees or the beam once you finally locate the flashlight, your entire outlook on the world changes. You can finally see your way to that light. It's the same in our relationship with God.

Read Matthew 5:14-16. The contrast between light and dark is used often throughout the New Testament. Things that are evil, or of the world, are often referred to as being in darkness. The things of God are said to be light. Jesus tells us that those who follow Him are the light of the world. We are not to try to hide this fact, but in actuality, are to let it shine brightly for others to see.

The world is full of people living in darkness, those who don't know Jesus and can find God on their own. They can spend their whole lives on the broad road wandering aimlessly toward destruction. As a follower of the Christ, your light, your good works done out of your love for Jesus, serve as a beacon, a signal flare showing others how to find the way to life.

Wouldn't you like to lead people living in darkness to the bright shining light of Jesus Christ?

Who served as a light in your life to show you the Way?

What does it mean for us to let our light shine before others?

How do our good works serve to point others to God?

Write a prayer below asking for God's help in letting your light shine brightly. Thank Him for those in your life He has used as light to show you the Way.

verse

> "I have set you an example that yo
> should do as I have done for you
> (John 13:15

hat was the last new skill you learned? Maybe it was to play the guit
or change the oil in your car. Perhaps you learned to bake your favorite dessert
design a web page. Some people are blessed with the gift of being able to teac
themselves how to do things. They can read instructions and know immediately ho
to do whatever it is they're reading. Some people don't even need instructions!

However, for most people that's not the case. The vast majority need to be taught ho
to do things, and to have someone patiently walk them through each step of the wa
Through the personal and faithful instruction of the teacher, combined with diligen
practice and rehearsal, expertise slowly grows over time. And eventually, the learne
gains the ability to become a teacher to someone else.

Read John 13:13-17. During His final night with His disciples before His arrest, Jesu
washed the disciples' feet, an act of humility unheard of for a teacher to perform fo
his followers. Jesus did this not just to teach the disciples a lesson or to reveal H
grace to them, but also to set them an example. He had us in mind, as well.

The Way is a way of service. All of us are called to serve each other. This isn't a skill tha
comes naturally. It's one we develop over time through a lot of practice. The more w
serve, the more we become like our Teacher, the Master who came not to be serve
but to serve others.

We will never become greater than Christ. But through our example, we will be abl
to teach others the servant's Way.

What does it mean to live a life of service?

In what ways do you currently serve others?

How are you involved in continuing to follow Jesus' example and be an example
to others?

Write a prayer below thanking Jesus for showing us the Way and providing an example
for us to emulate. Ask Him to continue to reveal to you ways in which you might
serve others.

verse 9

> "But when he, the Spirit of truth, comes, he will guide you into all truth. He will not speak on his own; he will speak only what he hears, and he will tell you what is yet to come."
>
> (John 16:13)

Think for just a moment about what it would be like for you to have to leave all the people you care about. Imagine you are leaving, going somewhere they can't go. And you're going to be gone a really long time. Before you leave, they're going to throw a huge going away party. So at the party, everyone's having a great time . . . eating, laughing, having fun. Suddenly, your best friend stands up. Everyone quiets down. Your friend asks you to give a speech. Here's your last chance to say whatever you want to those closest to you before you're whisked away. What would you say?

Read John 16:7-15. These are some of the last words Jesus had with His disciples before He was arrested and ultimately crucified. He knew that He would be leaving this world for the next. He had come to show all humankind the Way, yet there was still so much that He had to tell them, to tell us. However, He still said that His leaving was a good thing. Why? Because when He went away, the Counselor would come—another helper for us on our journey through life.

So, who is this Counselor? He is the Holy Spirit. Jesus called Him the Spirit of Truth and said that when the Spirit came, He would convict the world of guilt in regard to sin and righteousness and judgment and guide followers of Christ into all truth. He would be able to do so because He doesn't speak on His own. The Spirit speaks directly on behalf of Jesus and the Father. Jesus cares deeply about each one of us and knew we'd need some assistance along the path. So, He didn't leave any of us alone on the Way to figure it out as we go along. He sent us a helper, a guide for our journey, the Spirit of Truth.

reflect

1. What do you know about the Holy Spirit?

2. What questions do you have about the Holy Spirit?

3. How does the Bible teach that the Spirit will guide us in life?

4. Write a prayer below thanking Jesus for asking the Father to send the Spirit. Ask the Spirit to continue to fulfill His role in your life by guiding you into all truth and revealing to you what is yet to come.

verse

"Therefore go and make disciples of all
nations, baptizing them in the name
of the Father and of the Son and of the
Holy Spirit."
(Matt. 28:19)

How would you define the word purpose? Let's define it here as a goal, or the intended outcome of something. So, what is your purpose in life? Do you have goals, things you really want to do or accomplish while you're here on Earth? What are they?

Often, purpose is a difficult concept to nail down. There may be any number of reasons for this, but one is that a purpose isn't easy to distinguish. It's not simple. It's complex. Multiple goals or outcomes might go into defining the singular purpose of a person or thing. For instance, what is the purpose of fire? Is its purpose to consume its fuel? Is it to provide heat? Is it to cook something? Is its purpose to provide light? Anyone who's been camping knows that a campfire's purpose includes all four of these aspects.

Taking that into account, what then is our purpose on the Way?

Read Matthew 28:18-20. Jesus had all authority in the universe. He could have given the disciples any task. So, what did Jesus instruct them to do? He commanded them to make other disciples, to tell people about Him, to baptize people and teach them everything they had learned.

The disciples found their purpose on the Way. So do we today. The life to which the narrow Way leads is a life of meaning. The Way is not just meant for the individual person walking along, but for the world. Those of us who are the "few," who found the Way through the small gate, are tasked with making sure that everyone we meet knows about it and is given the chance to enter it as well.

reflect

. What goals do you have for your life?

. How does Jesus' purpose for your life affect your own goals?

. How are you currently involved in making disciples? How can you become
more involved?

. Write a prayer below expressing your gratitude to Jesus for giving your life meaning and
purpose. Ask Him to continually reveal how to better make disciples along the Way.

verse 11

> "About that time there arose a great disturbance about the Way"
> (Acts 19:23)

Imagine this scenario: It's a perfect summer day, and you have it all planned out. You sleep late. Once you get up, you call your friends and make plans to go to the lake. After a day of waterskiing, you go pick up that certain someone for dinner, surprising them with front row tickets to see your favorite band. The best part? You can stay out as long as you want. No curfew.

Sounds awesome, right? What if the scenario went like this:

Your dog wakes you up early, and you can't go back to sleep. Your mom needs the car. Your friends are already at the lake and can't come get you. You go to meet your crush only to find out the crush's little brother has to tag along. You end up giving the two of them the tickets. Since you don't have a curfew, you go to the late showing of that new movie, trying to salvage at least part of your day. But when you get home, your dad insists he never said you could stay out that late. You're grounded for a month.

Pretty disturbing, huh? Read Acts 19:23-27. The Way is still disturbing. It is a completely different way of living from how the world tells us to live. When we choose the narrow path of Christ, our lives are completely disturbed. But it is not just our lives.

As we live in ways that bring honor and glory to Christ, we make a disturbance in the world. This life on the Way does not go unnoticed. We'll be observed, talked about, and sometimes even plotted against, all because the Way continues to cause a great disturbance, even today.

reflect

1. How has your life been disturbed because of your choice to walk the narrow path of Christ?

2. In what ways does a life lived for Jesus cause a disturbance in the world?

3. Taking that into account, how then has your life caused a disturbance in the world?

4. Write a prayer below thanking God for disturbing your life and not allowing you to continue on the broad road to destruction. Pray for His strength and guidance when others get angry at you for disturbing their world because of your faithfulness to the Way.

verse 12

> "They devoted themselves to the apostles' teaching and to the fellowship, to the breaking of bread and to prayer."
> (Acts 2:42)

If you had to label your group of friends with a descriptive name based on how other people perceive you, what would it be? Maybe you're the Artsy Geniuses or the Athletic Models. You could be the God Squad, the Gamer Junkies, or the Fashionistas. Perhaps your group is a bit more complex like the Urban Bull-Riding Skater Nerds or the AP Footballer Scenester Movie Buffs. Maybe you dislike labels altogether and try to hang out with as many different people as possible. Regardless of who you hang out with, the reality is that you are probably known for something, and what you're known for inevitably has a lot to do with how you look, talk, and act.

Read Acts 2:42-47. The early followers of the Way "enjoyed the favor of all the people." This means people actually kind of liked them. This was because of who they were, what they said, and how they acted. The followers of the Way wanted to learn as much as they could. So they listened to everything the apostles had to say about Jesus. They hung out with each other. They ate together and had a good time, and they prayed—a lot—for each other and for other people.

Now think about your church and your youth group. You can follow the examples of your early brothers and sisters. You have the teaching of the apostles written in the Bible. You have times set aside throughout the week to be able to meet together. Not only that, but you don't have to spend time together just at church. You can go out together, be seen and be proud of who you are and whom you follow. And, of course, you can pray—a lot—for each other and for other people.

1. What do people think about your church or your youth group, good or bad?

2. Why do people have those perceptions?

3. What role do you play in contributing to those perceptions?

4. Write a prayer below thanking God for the example of the early followers of the Way. Ask Him to reveal how you might lead your group in finding favor among all the people because of your obedience to their example.

verse 13

"All the believers were one in heart and mind. No one claimed that any of his possessions was his own, but they shared everything they had."

(Acts 4:32)

Everyone loves getting gifts. Birthdays. Christmas. Valentines. A person's entire face lights up at the sight of a wrapped present just waiting to be opened. However, some of us get as much satisfaction out of giving someone a gift as we do out of receiving one. Are you like that? People who really like to give gifts think hard about what someone would like. They see something in a store and think immediately of a friend who can't live without it. They'll go to great lengths to get it for them, and then they'll try to work out the perfect way to surprise them with it. If you're not one of those people for whom giving comes naturally, you need to try it more often. You'll quickly find how easy it is to develop a passion for it.

Read Acts 4:32-35. The early Church was growing exponentially in the early chapters of Acts. More and more people were choosing the narrow Way, and they came from all walks of life: young and old, male and female, Jew and Gentile, rich and poor. Not only did they find favor with people outside the Church, but they liked each other as well. Actually, they genuinely loved each other. So, whenever a fellow follower of the Way needed something, they would simply make sure the need was met. They were so devoted to each other that the giving just came naturally.

The world tells us that it's every man for himself and that we should look out for number one. The Way tells us that we're responsible for each other and that our love should always lead to sharing and giving.

reflect

What is the best reaction you've ever had to a gift? How do you think your reaction made the person who gave you that gift feel?

What needs do you know others have that you can help provide for?

What does it mean not to consider any possessions your own? Whose are they?

Write a prayer of thanks below to God for all the many ways in which He provides for you. Ask Him to reveal needs that others have around you and to show you how He might use you to provide for them.

"And when he found him, he brough
him to Antioch. So for a whole yea
Barnabas and Saul met with th
church and taught great number
of people. The disciples were calle
Christians first at Antioch
(Acts 11:26

Most people have heroes in their lives, people they look up to. Do you?

There may be someone in your life right now that you look up to, someone you kno
personally. But when you were a kid, your heroes were probably a little more fantasti
They might have been superheroes, like Rogue or the Green Lantern. They migh
have been your favorite character from a movie or book like Frodo or Harriet the Sp
Perhaps you wanted to be like someone from history, such as Davy Crockett or Amel
Earhart. Or maybe a celebrity. Regardless of who it was (or is), you probably spen
hours trying to be like them. You might have dressed like them, talked like them, eve
acted like them. You probably even imagined adventures and scenarios in which yo
could actually become, if only in your own mind, just like your hero.

Read Acts 11:25-26. Barnabas and Paul's lives were rocked because they decided t
follow the narrow Way. Barnabas had been on the path for a little longer than Paul an
decided to drag Paul to Antioch so that they could witness firsthand what was goin
on at the church there. What happened next was quite amazing.

See, the church in Antioch really listened to what Paul and Barnabas had to say. The
took their teaching to heart and actually began to live it. They became such devote
followers of Christ that people began calling them "Christians," a word that literall
means *little Christs*. They looked, talked, and acted so much like Jesus that whenever
others looked at them, people saw Christ.

Followers of the Way have sought to live up to their example ever since. What abou
you? Do people look at you and see Christ?

reflect

. What does it mean to be called a "Christian" if you are a follower of the narrow Way?

. What do you think it takes for someone to look at you and see Christ?

. "Christian" was a name given to the Antiochian believers after they spent a year studying and learning. What must you do in order to continue to grow into being more and more Christlike?

. Write a prayer below expressing your desire to become more like Christ. Ask God to reveal areas where you need to continue to grow.

verse 15

"But if it is from God, you will not be able to stop these men; you will only find yourselves fighting against God"

(Acts 5:39)

"You're either with us or against us." That's a powerful statement. There's no middle ground, no room for neutrality. You're either an ally or an enemy, and that's just the way it is. Maybe you're not really doing or saying anything actively in opposition, but by doing nothing at all, you are declaring your side.

This phrase, or something like it, is used throughout history. Recently it has been used when discussing the War on Terror. In Beauty and the Beast, Gaston uses it as an excuse to lock up Belle and her father so that he can go hunt the beast. Even Jesus said something similar in Matthew 12, Mark 9, and Luke 11.

Read Acts 5:27-42. We already know that the Way had been causing quite a disturbance. The apostles were leading more people to Christ every day. So, the Sanhedrin (the Jewish religious court) brought the apostles to trial to answer for what they were doing. The apostles' commitment to making disciples of the entire world enraged the religious elite. The Sanhedrin wanted to kill the apostles.

However, the Sanhedrin were stopped by one of their own, a respected leader named Gamaliel. He encouraged them to take a neutral position and to wait and see what happened. Israel's history was full of visionary leaders whose revolutions collapsed after their death. Once Jesus was killed, the only way His followers would succeed would be if Jesus were actually God's Son. It would only succeed if the apostles were doing the work of God.

Of course they were, and there was no stopping them. And there's no stopping us today.

. What does it mean to either be with someone or against them?

. How does this idea apply to our following Christ or not following Him?

. How does it feel that as a follower of the Way, you are part of an unstoppable movement of God?

. Write a prayer below telling God that you are with Him. Thank Him for allowing you to be a part of what He is doing in the world. Ask for confidence when it seems as if the world will win.

verse

"I have been crucified with Christ and
I no longer live, but Christ lives in me.
The life I live in the body, I live by faith
in the Son of God, who loved me and
gave himself for me."
(Gal. 2:20)

What gets you up in the morning? What do you look forward to in life? What motivates you as you start each day?

Your answer might depend on what day it is. On some days, you might look forward to seeing someone. On others, you could have the opportunity to do something you really love. You could just be tired of sleeping. Or maybe you're counting down each day to some future event that you can't wait for. Or the reason you get up in the morning might not even be something you think about at all.

Regardless of whether you realize it, all kinds of factors can motivate you through life.

Read Galatians 2:19-21. Obviously, when we choose the narrow Way our lives are completely changed, so much that Paul writes that we have died along with Christ, died to sin. Before we began to follow Christ, sin ruled our lives. But now that we have begun to follow Him, we live a life made possible by His sacrifice for us on the cross. Through our faith in Him, we live a new life in a new way.

We no longer have to work every day to try to get things right, to try to please God, or even to try to make the most of our lives. God makes us right with Him through Christ. He is pleased when we walk with Him along the Way daily. He makes the most of our lives by showing us a more perfect way. Since we don't have to worry about those things, our lives are motivated by something else: His love and sacrifice for us. Jesus lives in us as we live completely for Him.

What gets you up in the morning?

How does (or doesn't) this match up with your new life in Christ?

How do the love of Christ and His sacrifice for us on the cross motivate your life?

Write a prayer below thanking God that sin no longer reigns in your life. Ask Him to help you live a life completely dependent on your faith in Him through Jesus. Commit to reflect on His love for you as you live life each day.

verse 17

"Do not conform any longer to the pattern of this world, but be transformed by the renewing of your mind. Then you will be able to test and approve what God's will is—his good, pleasing and perfect will."
(Rom. 12:2)

"What is God's will for my life?" People ask this question all the time. If you've never asked it, get ready. It's inevitable. As our choices become more important to us, we can find ourselves scrambling, desperate to make the right decision, doing everything in our power to try to figure out just what God wants us to do.

Sometimes this actually helps us focus. Weighing our choices against God's Word can often provide insight so that we're able to eliminate at least a few options. However, at other times looking for the answer to God's will for our lives can paralyze us so that we can't do anything. We end up not making any decision at all out of complete fear that we won't get it right. This isn't how God wants us to live.

Read Romans 12:1-2. One of the first things to realize is that our lives on the Way are completely out of control, or at least out of *our* control. Paul tells the Roman Christians (and us) that the best way to live a worshipful life—one that is honoring and pleasing to God—is to live a life of sacrifice, where we give up our control and turn everything completely over to God. When we do this, we begin to live differently, not according to how the world wants us to live.

The world says, "You've got to look out for yourself. Your destiny is yours to make. It's all up to you." But along the Way, God transforms us completely from how we used to be, and we become how He intended us to be. As He transforms us, we start to understand His ways more and more. So the question of God's will for our lives may not always be simple to find, but the more time we spend with Him along the Way, the easier it is to recognize.

reflect

If you had to name right now what God's will is for your life, what would you say?

How do you know?

What do you think it means to be transformed through the renewing of your mind?

Write a prayer below asking God to continue the transformation process in you. Commit to Him that you will live sacrificially. Ask for His help in resisting the temptations of this world. Thank Him for having a will for your life that is good, pleasing, and perfect.

18

> "See to it that no one takes you captive through hollow and deceptive philosophy, which depends on human tradition and the basic principles of this world rather than on Christ"
>
> (Col. 2:8)

Think for a moment about going to a carnival or your state fair. Usually, you'll find all kinds of rides there—Ferris wheel, pirate ship, bumper cars, and the rest. Now get past the rides for a minute, and think about the midway—the long stretch right through the middle of everything.

Normally, in addition to rides, the midway has a ton of things going on. Carts are there selling elephant ears, chicken-on-a-stick, Polish sausages, and funnel cakes. You can find any number of games to play and prizes to win. Workers try to guess your age or your weight in exchange for a couple of bucks. And then there are mysterious tents, which promise all kinds of wonders inside. A tent might hold the world's largest alligator or proof of alien life on Mars, a full-sized house carved out of a pumpkin or an African pigmy princess. Regardless, if you ever actually buy a ticket and venture inside looking for wonder, you'll find that it never lives up to its promise.

Read Colossians 2:6-8. Paul encouraged the church at Colosse (and us today) to continue to live in Christ. He knew that simply choosing the narrow Way wasn't a one-time deal. The journey is continuing. He also knew that along the Way, some people would try to lead us astray. Evil forces at work in the world want nothing more than to keep followers of Christ distracted. Though we are set free and are no longer slaves to sin, these forces want to take us captive again through their way of thinking—thoughts based purely on what we are capable of rather than on Christ. Like the phony promises made at a midway tent, people will try and lead us astray along the Way. You have to be constantly aware and learn to avoid being taken in.

How do we do this? By being rooted in Christ, secure and strengthened in Him and His teachings.

reflect

What are some hollow or deceptive philosophies that you know about?

Why can these other ways of living be so tempting, even leading some followers of Christ astray?

How can you avoid being led astray yourself?

Write a prayer below committing yourself to remaining rooted in Christ and continuing to live in Him. Ask God to help you recognize empty promises and learn how to avoid them. Repent of any ways in which you might have already been led astray.

verse 19

"Your attitude should be the same a[s]
that of Christ Jesus...[ ]
(Phil. 2:5[)]

magine coming home from school one day when things have not gone you[r] way. You were late. You had a pop quiz. For some reason, your locker wouldn't oper[ ]At lunch, you spilled your drink all over your shirt. You found out someone's bee[n] spreading a rumor about you. You forgot to bring that extra-credit assignment tha[t] you actually did this time. And to top it all off, you discovered that certain someon[e] already has a date this weekend. In other words, it's been a bad day.

You got home and walked in the door. Your mom was in the kitchen, and she said, "H[i] honey, how was your day?" You snapped. You just couldn't take it. You knew that sh[e] had nothing to do with your bad day, but you really let her have it. When you wer[e] done, you could tell she was upset. Then she said what she always says when that kin[d] of thing happens. "You need an attitude adjustment."

Read Philippians 2:1-11. Your mom's right. You do need an attitude adjustment. We a[ll] do. It's natural for us to be selfish. But we don't walk along the narrow Way alone. We'r[e] joined by all kinds of other people trying to live in Christ just as we are. Some of them we get along with great. Others, we don't. Regardless, God calls us to care about eac[h] other more than ourselves.

This is the attitude that Jesus has. He is God, yet He chose to become human and liv[e] on Earth. If ever a person deserved to be concerned with only themselves, it was Him[.] But He wasn't. He chose to live as a servant, caring for everyone regardless of wh[o] they were or what else He had going on in His life. We're called to do the same thing.

reflect

1. Define the word attitude.

2. What does it mean for someone to be in need of an attitude adjustment?

3. How can you adjust (or how have you adjusted) your own attitude?

4. Write a prayer below thanking Jesus for taking the nature of a servant. Ask for God's help in placing others' needs above your own. Pray for a continued adjustment of your attitude into that of Christ Jesus.

"And this is love: that we walk in obedience to his commands. As you have heard from the beginning, his command is that you walk in love."
(2 John 1:6)

We use the word love to describe the way we feel about all kinds of things. We love our parents. We love our dog. We love God. We love sports or music or fashion or camping. We love movies. We love texting, IMing, or poking. We love our significant other and pizza and ice cream and sleeping in. Some of us might even love going to school (though most of us probably don't). You get the picture.

While we can really like each of these things, even to the point of saying we love them, we don't feel the same way about all of them. You don't love your mom like you love football like you love pizza like you love God. At least I hope you don't. But because we use this one word, love, to describe how we feel about so many things, nailing down just what we mean can be difficult.

Read 2 John 1:5-6. The Apostle John wrote this letter to a certain lady he knew. Within it are themes common to the rest of John's writings, and one theme emerges in particular. Love.

John was always admonishing people to love. He knew that Jesus had taught them that the world would know that we are His followers by our love. He placed incredible value on loving others and living a loving life. As John said, from the beginning, if nothing else followers of Jesus knew that they were to walk in love. But just what is this love he spoke about? It's walking in obedience to what God has told us through His Word. When we are obedient, we show our love for God to Him and to others. Our lives look different. And since He is love, when we do what He says, we inevitably end up having that same love flow through us. That is the way to walk, the way to live. The Way of love.

reflect

1. Make a list of all of the different things that you would say you love.

2. Now, taking that list into account, what does the word love mean to you?

3. According to what you know about the Bible, what do you think love means to God?

4. Write a prayer below asking God to transform your understanding of love into His understanding of it. Pray for strength to live a life that is obedient to God's commands. Ask forgiveness for when you have failed to live a loving life recently. Commit to continue walking in love.

21 verse

"To the weak I became weak, to win the weak. I have become all things to all men so that by all possible means I might save some."
(1 Cor. 9:22)

Consider all the people you encounter at your school or mall or swimming pool or park. Imagine for a moment each individual person. Imagine how they look and how they dress. Envision the way they stand and how they walk. Pretty soon, you realize just how incredibly different each one of us really is.

Think about your group of friends. What makes you all hang out together? Chances are that you share something in common. It might be something you do, like a sport. It might be something you're interested in, like movies. Maybe what unites you is that you've all grown up together. Perhaps you're all going to the same college next year. So, you're embarking on a new adventure together. The point is that something common among you unites you together.

Now, picture your friends combined with all the people you imagined at the beginning of this devotion. A diverse group, right? Now go bigger. Consider all the people in your town, or in this country, or even in the world. What do we all have in common? What unites all 6.6 billion of us as human beings?

Read 1 Corinthians 9:19-23. The Apostle Paul knew what it meant to walk the Way in love. He genuinely cared about other people. He had the gift of looking at a group of people and recognizing a common factor that united them all. He also examined his own life and saw what he might share with them. Paul would then focus on those common characteristics—what made them more alike than different. In doing so, he was able to actually find an effective and compassionate way of communicating the good news of Christ to them.

The Way can take a lot of work, but if you will imitate the concern Paul showed for others, you might find you're capable of being just as effective at sharing your faith.

reflect

1. What common experiences unite all people, regardless of where they live?

2. Why should we concern ourselves with becoming "all things to all people"?

3. Who are some people you know who need to hear the gospel of Christ? How can you become "like them" in order to share this good news with them?

4. Write a prayer below thanking Jesus for becoming like us in order to bring the gospel to Earth. Ask for insight in knowing how best to talk with other people about this good news.

verse

"Therefore let us stop passing
judgment on one another.
Instead, make up your mind not
to put any stumbling block or
obstacle in your brother's way."
(Rom. 14:13)

The next time you're driving around, try to notice the names of all the churches in your city. Most will display what kind of church they are by listing what denomination they are. You will see Baptist churches and Methodist churches. Catholic and Anglican. Presbyterian and Lutheran. Pentecostal and African Methodist Episcopalian. Some churches won't be affiliated with a denomination at all.

Members of these churches would each tell you they are followers of Christ. However, each church would differ from another on various issues—some petty and others significant. Face it: Christians can disagree on exactly what we believe. Because of this, it's important for us to find common ground. We should discuss any significant differences so that we can challenge each other as to what is truth. But what should we do about the little things?

Read Romans 14:13-18. When Paul was writing to the church in Rome, he knew people walking the narrow Way would have disagreements on issues. In his letters, Paul sought to help answer some of the big issues. But in these verses, he gave us some insight into how to handle the small ones. His advice? Don't let small issues come between you and your brothers and sisters in Christ.

You can have questions about all kinds of things: Should you only listen to certain music? What movies or television shows should you watch? Is it OK to go to particular parties? What language is inappropriate for a follower of Christ? Should you be allowed to date? Yet along the Way, you need to be a help to others, not a hindrance. So, whenever you learn about issues that fellow followers of Christ have, whether or not they seem petty to you, your goal should not be to use these differences to judge or condemn. The idea is to distinguish the major issues from the minor ones.

reflect

1. What are some big issues that followers of Christ may disagree on that we should discuss in order to challenge each other as to the truth?

2. What are some small issues that can not only hang us up, but also cause unnecessary conflict with fellow followers of Christ?

3. How can you avoid making these small issues stumbling blocks or obstacles in the lives of others?

4. Write a prayer below asking God for wisdom and discernment in recognizing the issues you can help avoid making an obstacle for others. Ask Him to continue to unite His followers around the world.

verse 23

> "Carry each other's burdens, and
> in this way you will fulfill the law
> of Christ."
> (Gal. 6:2)

It can be really tough to watch a friend who is going through a difficult time. They could be struggling with a disease or a habitual sin. Someone close to them may have died. Their parents could be getting divorced. Maybe it's just that their grades at school aren't what they used to be, or they didn't get what they tried out for. Regardless of the specifics, it really stinks. Not just for them, but for you, too.

It's hard to know exactly what to say or how you're supposed to act, especially if you've never been in a similar situation. You want to help, but try as you might, nothing really seems to work. You can even get to the point where you're so frustrated that you don't do anything at all, just ignoring the problem until everything gets back to normal. Or so you hope.

Read Galatians 6:1-5. Obviously, each of us is responsible for our own life, even though we don't always act like it. However, the issue here is that when your friend is struggling through life, whether it's their fault or not, you can't just sit back and watch them go through it. Instead, you're called to walk through it with them.

This is yet another aspect that makes the narrow Way difficult. Why? Because when you walk through life's problems with someone, you don't just tag along beside them. You actually help them carry their burden in whatever way you can. This doesn't mean that you always have to have the right answers or know exactly what to do. But it does mean that you are right there with them asking questions and searching for the next step.

. Whom do you know right now that is struggling through a difficult time?

. How can you help bear their burden?

. What people have been there in your life to help bear your burdens?

. Write a prayer below thanking God for those people who have helped you along the Way. Ask for His wisdom in helping bear the burdens of others you know that need help.

verse

> "I can do everything through him who gives me strength"
> (Phil. 4:13)

Every little boy has a point in life when he wants to be Superman. In fact, chances are that he even spent at least one whole Saturday wearing his Superman Underoos®, a blue t-shirt, and a red towel or bed sheet tied around his neck like a cape. If he was really unfortunate (or just stupid), the day might have ended with a trip to the hospital after he jumped off the roof thinking just maybe he could actually fly.

So what is it about Superman that appeals to so many people? Well, he's a man, and he's super. He can do practically anything, right? He's faster than a speeding bullet, more powerful than a locomotive, and able to leap tall buildings in a single bound. He can fly. He has heat and x-ray vision. He can even turn back time by reversing the rotation of the Earth. He's nearly invincible. And where does all of this superpower come from? Well, answers to that question have been somewhat varied over the years. However, the most commonly accepted explanation is that his powers are made possible through radiation from our yellow sun.

Read Philippians 4:10-14. The Apostle Paul knew what it was like to have problems. He experienced a lot of trouble and persecution. But he also knew what it was like to have the support of other followers of the Way. He knew how important it was not only to be supported by others, but also for others to have the opportunity to lend their support.

However, Paul had also learned the secret of getting through those times even when he didn't have that support. He could rely on a source of strength that was ever-present and never-changing. God was always there for him, strengthening and supporting him. He's also there for us in the same way.

God gives you the kind of power each day that superheroes could only dream about.

If you could be granted one superpower, what would it be?

How does God strengthen us?

At what times in your life have you really had to rely on God's strength?

Write a prayer below asking God for His strength in difficult times. Thank Him for strengthening you through those times in the past even if you didn't know it. Ask Him to help you continue to find contentment in life.

"Do not be yoked together
with unbelievers. For what do
righteousness and wickedness have
in common? Or what fellowship can
light have with darkness?
(2 Cor. 6:14

"Ah, the three-legged race. It's a staple of county fairs, family reunion
elementary school field days, and youth groups everywhere. You know the drill .
Two people pair up. One person's leg is attached to the leg of another person wit
anything from a piece of rope to a full-length Velcro® leg support. The tied-togeth
pair goes to the starting line with all the other pairs and waits for the signal.

"On your mark. Get set. Go!" All the pairs hobble toward the finish line. Some pai
are really working together. Others are lying in a heap. Still others have one perso
dragging the other along. Eventually, one pair makes it to the finish line and
announced the winner while everyone else rejoices that the game is finally over.

Anyone who has ever run a three-legged race knows that the secret to winning is th
getting the right partner.

Read 2 Corinthians 6:14-7:1. Throughout the Bible, God admonishes His people to b
holy, to be separate from the world. In fact, the word translated most often in the Ne
Testament as church literally means "those called out." This implies a group of peop
separate from something else. So, what are the implications for our relationships wi
people who aren't followers of Christ? The secret is in the word yoked. The pictu
here is of two oxen working together to pull a cart or plow. If one ox were strong
than the other, the work wouldn't get done. In fact, the weaker ox would keep th
stronger one from fulfilling its potential.

This verse doesn't mean that you shouldn't associate at all with people who are o
the wide path. It simply means that your close relationships, your partnerships
life, have to be with people seeking the same destination as you—those walking th
narrow Way.

reflect

What do you think it means to be "yoked" together with an unbeliever?

In what ways is that different from being friends with them? Or is it different?

How have you been called out from the world?

Write a prayer below asking God to help you navigate the relationships in your life. Commit to live a life separate from the world even while you live in it. Thank God for the other followers of Christ with whom you are currently yoked.

verse

> "Submit yourselves, then, to
> God. Resist the devil, and he will
> flee from you.
> (James 4:7)

An archenemy is the principal foe of the hero in a work of fiction. The enemy is the hero's worst adversary. His rival. His nemesis. The antagonist to the protagonist. There are many we're familiar with. Think about it: Little Red Riding Hood has the Big Bad Wolf. The Pevensie children from The Lion, the Witch, and the Wardrobe have the White Witch. Captain Jack Sparrow has Davy Jones. Superman has Lex Luthor. Batman has the Joker. The survivors of Oceanic Flight 815 have the Others.

Read James 4:7-10. God has an archenemy as well, sometimes referred to as the enemy. He's Satan, the devil. God and Satan stand in direct opposition to each other. God desires to save the world. Satan wants to destroy it. God is love. Satan is hate. God humbled Himself, taking on the nature of a servant. Satan basks in his pride and seeks to bring everyone under his dominion. God is the Author of truth. Satan is the father of lies. The list could go on.

When you choose to follow the narrow Way, God sets you free from sin's power. However, He doesn't then leave things up to you. You are called to submit yourself to Him and His authority in your life. This is the picture of soldiers submitting themselves to the command of their officer. You see, in reality a spiritual war is raging around us. When you join God's mission in the world, Satan becomes your enemy as well. As you continue to submit to and follow God, you are enabled to resist, or stand up against the devil. When you do, Scripture says he will flee from you.

Part of the reason that the Way is difficult is that you come under constant attack. But as you humble yourself before God, He will raise you up to be victorious. You are promised victory. It's already decided by Christ's death and resurrection.

1. What are some other great archenemies that you can think of from movies or literature?

2. Is there a person in your life that you might have at one point considered to be—or even now consider to be—your archenemy?

3. What does it mean for you to know that your struggles along the Way are actually not with other people but with evil forces working around you?

4. Write a prayer below thanking God for the victory over sin and death through Jesus Christ. Pray for the future victory that is even yet to come. Commit to continue in submission to God and ask for His help in standing against Satan when he comes against you.

> "Consider it pure joy, my brothers,
> whenever you face trials of many
> kinds…"
> (James 1:2)

Do you know anyone who is a workout fiend? You know, the kind of person who can think of nothing better than waking up before school to jog a couple of miles? They navigate the halls of your school as if they're in a speed-walking race. Their wardrobe consists of mostly Under Armour®. They spend their afternoons at a gym and say things like, "No pain, no gain," and "Come on. Work it out." They absolutely love it. Maybe you're one of those people.

For many people, this type of joy in working out doesn't come naturally. In fact, many people can think of nothing they'd like to do less than go run around a track or pump some iron at the gym. Sure, they don't mind taking a walk or getting in a good swim. That can be fun. But the minute there is any level of discomfort, you can count them out. A lot of times people approach their spiritual lives the same way.

Read James 1:2-4. It is already completely apparent that the narrow Way is often hard. You know that you will have struggles and will come under constant attack. There may be any number of obstacles you must overcome. However, that doesn't mean you have to be happy about it, right? Actually, that's pretty much wrong.

The trials you encounter along the Way play a very important role in your life. The more you are tested, the more perseverance you develop—just as the more you work out, the more muscle tone and stamina you have. God knows life often isn't easy. He knows it's a marathon and not a sprint. You need a great deal of perseverance to get through it.

While perseverance comes from working through difficult times, the results are well worth it.

reflect

1. How difficult is it to be joyful when you face trials in life?

2. What does it mean to persevere through something?

3. How does perseverance work toward making you mature and complete?

4. Write a prayer below asking God to teach you what it means to have joy in life's trials. Thank Him for using difficult times to produce perseverance within you. Commit to continuing to persist even through struggles.

28 verse

"Therefore, since we are surrounded by such a great cloud of witnesses, let us throw off everything that hinders and the sin that so easily entangles, and let us run with perseverance the race marked out for us."
(Heb. 12:1)

Most people, at some point in their lives, have imagined what it would be like to bask in the adoration of thousands of fans. You probably have, too. Maybe you thought about what it would be like to kick the winning goal in the last seconds of the final game of the World Cup. You could have wondered how it would feel to take a victory lap after winning the Daytona 500. Perhaps you've always dreamed of giving a concert at Madison Square Garden or accepting an Academy Award®.

Whatever situation you thought of for yourself, it inevitably involved a moment where your greatness was recognized by everyone present. All attention was focused on you. The crowd rose to their feet. Thunderous applause and deafening cheers followed. As you pictured the scene, you might have even mimicked what you hoped to hear by cupping your hand around your mouth and breathily cheering yourself. Though not the real thing, the very hope of such a time might have been enough to maintain a feeling of exhilaration throughout the day.

Read Hebrews 11:39-12:3. The Way is a path that has been blazed before you. Jesus came to Earth to reveal it. Throughout history, God has guided His people through each step they took. For those of us on the Way, we have become a part of His grand plan. As you race along, sometimes sprinting—other times crawling, weighed down by your sin and struggles—all those who have gone before cheer you on through the testimony of their lives on the Way. You're able to keep your focus ahead on Christ. When you finally reach the joy set before you, your life will stand as a testimony to others, cheering them on as well.

1. Who are some "heroes of the faith" that have blazed the Way for you, people you really look up to?

2. How has the testimony of their lives encouraged you along the Way?

3. What keeps you going when you feel weary in life?

4. Write a prayer below thanking God for all of the witnesses that surround you and for the testimony of their lives. Commit to run with perseverance. Ask God to continue developing your life into one that is a testimony to others.

verse

"Do not merely listen to the word, and so deceive yourselves. Do what it says."
(James 1:22)

Colin, a teenage guy, sits at a café across from his girlfriend, April. They've been together since junior high. He says he really loves her. April tells Colin how much her feelings are hurt because he wanted to go camping with the guys instead of to her dance showcase. She's been talking for the past half hour. Colin really hasn't said much of anything. He just kind of stares at her, takes a sip of his drink, a bite of his burger. He looks out the window. He snaps out of it when April lunges forward over the table and says, "Colin, are you really listening to me?"

Now Colin *heard* everything April said. The sound waves traveled from her mouth into his ear. They were processed by his brain as sound and interpreted as words he understood. April obviously knew this. So, what did she mean when she asked if he was really listening to her?

Read James 1:22-25. There's a difference between hearing and acknowledging what a person says and actually responding to it. What April wants Colin to do is to understand where she's coming from and adjust his behavior in the future. He says he loves her. Shouldn't he want to do that?

How many of us treat God the way Colin was treating April? We read His Word to hear what He has to say to us, but then we don't really give a response.

God desires for your journey on the Way to be in a relationship with Him where you grow in your affection for Him and know Him increasingly better. As you do so, you are called to respond out of your love for and understanding of Him so that you may be completely transformed into what He wants you to be. Why would you want to do anything else?

1. What is the difference between merely hearing what someone says and really listening to them?

2. What is so difficult about doing what we hear in God's Word?

3. How is our lack of response to God's Word a way in which we deceive ourselves?

4. Write a prayer below thanking God for His Word. Commit to study it and to do what it says. Ask the Spirit to continue guiding you into the truth of God's Word and empowering you to live it.

VERSE

"Don't let anyone look down on you because you are young, but set an example for the believers in speech, in life, in love, in faith and in purity."
(1 Tim. 4:12)

"You're just a kid." "You'll understand better when you're older." "Hush now, honey, grown-ups are talking."

You are probably already fuming after reading those sentences. They bring to mind memories of being dismissed by someone older than you, not because you didn't know what you were talking about, but simply because you were a certain age. Now, hopefully you will continue to grow and mature the older you get. But does that mean you have to wait to reach some arbitrary age in order to be effective for the Kingdom of God?

Read 1 Timothy 4:9-14. If you're not careful, you can live your entire life in constant preparation for some event in the future. When you're in elementary school, you're just waiting for junior high—then high school, then your senior year, then college, then grad school or a career, then family, then retirement. Before you know it, you can be in your twilight years, looking back and wondering where the time went. That is not God's plan for you.

Timothy was younger than most of the people in the church he was charged with leading in Ephesus. However, his mentor, Paul, believed in him and knew that God wanted to use Timothy regardless of his age. Paul's encouragement to Timothy is good for you to hear. Your age shouldn't matter. The manner in which you live should. Don't let what people think of your age affect you.

Your challenge is to set an example for everyone around you. Show them how they should speak and the things they should talk about. Let them look at your life and see what it means to walk with God. Make it completely apparent that you are a follower of the Way by loving God and loving people. See that you remain untainted by the evils of this world.

Do these things, and no one will be able to dismiss you for any reason. Not even your age.

reflect

1. Why is it so easy for people to not listen to someone who is younger than they are?

2. In what ways do you think someone your age can help be an example in your local church?

3. How can you, personally, be an example for other believers?

4. Write a prayer below thanking God for wanting to use someone your age. Commit to be an example for other believers in speech, in life, in love, in faith and in purity. Ask for the power to be able to do so effectively.

31 verse

"Who is it that overcomes the world? Only he who believes that Jesus is the Son of God." (1 John 5:5)

"We Shall Overcome" is a key anthem from the American Civil Rights Movement. Its title and lyrics are taken from an old gospel tune dating back to the 1800s. The chorus for the song is simply, "Oh, deep in my heart/I do believe/We shall overcome/some day," and the verses include statements like, "We shall all be free," "We are not afraid," "We are not alone," and "We'll walk hand in hand."

Advocates of the civil rights movement saw the world as being against them, and in many ways it was. Yet they fought to overcome injustices that the world perpetrated upon them. It's no surprise, then, that for many of those involved in the movement, their faith in God was what sustained them.

Read 1 John 5:5. The Way is narrow. It is hard. Only a few find it. All along the Way you are under constant attack by the forces of evil that seek nothing but your destruction. Followers of the Way are called to live in direct opposition to how the world tells you to live. Along the Way, you will often stumble. It will seem like you have no idea where to go or what to do. You'll be judged, mocked and ridiculed. It will seem as if the whole world is against you.

When you are worn down and losing your resolve, when life seems hard enough without having to live so differently, when you are doing a lot more crawling than walking, and when you wonder if God really knows what He's doing, keep in mind you have something to hold on to. You know the secret of overcoming all of it: your faith. "Who is it that overcomes the world? Only he who believes that Jesus is the Son of God."

That is the Way to life.

1. What, according to the way you see it, makes the Way so difficult?

2. What struggles are you having along the Way right now?

3. How does it help you to know that you will overcome?

4. Write a prayer below confessing to God all the difficulties you are having along the Way. Ask for His continued strength and guidance to get through it. Thank Him for the promise that you will overcome.

closing

So, now what? You've finished this book (good for you, by the way), and hopefully God has used it to teach you a little more about the Way and to encourage you as you seek to walk a life along the narrow path. But what's next? Honestly, it's tough to say for sure. Each person's journey is unique. However, there are a few things you should probably keep in mind.

First, your journey on the Way is a lifelong endeavor. Don't think that it ends here or that you've figured it all out or learned everything you need to know. Keep growing in your faith. Spend a lot of time in God's Word. You don't need a book like this to help you with that. The Holy Spirit is with you. Pray constantly, continuously seeking God and His plan for your life.

Second, you're not in this alone. Not only is God ever-present with you at each step, but a lot of people are also walking the Way with you. Get together with some friends regularly just to talk about how things are going. Be open and honest with each other. Pray, and support the others in your group. Look for someone traveling the Way that you look up to. Ask them to make an investment in you, and to talk to you about their own experiences along the Way.

Last, don't give up. If there's anything that's guaranteed about life on the Way, it's that things aren't always going to be sunshine and rainbows. What you can be sure of, though, is that it's worth it. Jesus said that He came that we "may have life, and have it to the full." He came to show us the Way so that our lives here on Earth could be everything they could possibly be. That's the kind of life He wants you to live. You should want to live this life, too.

about the author

Chris Kinsley is a real-deal follower of the Way of Jesus Christ. He doesn't always get it right, but by the grace of God, he manages to continue along. Even though studying can really be a struggle, he somehow managed to get his Master of Divinity from Beeson Divinity School. He was once the youth associate at First Baptist Church in Jackson, Mississippi, and he currently serves as the Creative Producer for Student Life. That just means he gets to help come up with cool ideas for everything Student Life does. Can you believe they pay someone for that? Chris, his wife, Liza, and their dog, a Westie named Missy, currently reside in Helena, Alabama. You can find out more about him and read his blog at www.chriskinsley.com.

Executive Editor
Andy Blanks

Copy Editor
Lynn Groom

Art Director
Mike Robinson

Graphic Design
Zack Nichols

Publishing Assistant
Brooke Culpepper
Staci Caldwell

Studentlifestore.com...
isn't just for youth ministers.

Check out these resources, designed with teenagers in mind:

iPod Videos
Love the videos you watch at Camp, Tour, or in Student Life Bible Study? You can purchase special versions of these videos formatted especially for your iPod. Only $1.99 a piece.

31 Verses Every Teenager Should Know
These little books pack a big punch. This line of devotional books is written specifically with teenagers in mind. Learn how God's Word relates to your world through these fun, interactive, and informative line of resources.

Message Downloads
Whether there was a specific life-changing message at Camp or Tour, or you just want to be taught by some of the most dynamic speakers in the country, message downloads are just the thing for you.

There is much more waiting for you at studentlifestore.com.
Check it out today.